How to Receive Salvation and What to Do With It

Workbook

EDIFYING THE CHRISTIAN

Greg Magee

Copyright © 2025 by Gregory LaCrae Magee Jr.

All rights reserved. No part of this book may be used or reproduced in any manner whatsoever without written permission, except in the case of brief quotations embodied in critical articles and reviews. Direct your requests to the publisher.

Published by:
Edifying the Christian
www.edifyingthechristian.org

Printed in the United States of America, 2025.

Unless otherwise indicated, all Scripture quotations are taken from the Holy Bible, New Living Translation, copyright © 1996, 2004, 2015 by Tyndale House Foundation. Used by permission of Tyndale House Publishers, Inc., Carol Stream, Illinois 60188. All rights reserved.

About the Author

Greg Magee is a Georgia high school teacher. He enjoys teaching teamwork, communication, critical thinking, and problem-solving skills. He is a member of Cartersville First Baptist Church, which he attends with his wife and kids. He credits his parents for obeying God's Word in raising him.

Message from the Author

I was inspired to write this booklet by teenagers who wanted to know God, believe in Him, and be saved by Him. Some of them attended church regularly but didn't understand the reason for going. Others did not attend regularly and didn't see the need to. Many of my young friends had misconceptions about being saved and what to do after being saved. When I was their age, I did not fully understand the misconceptions many young people have shared with me. Now, I know the answers to many of the things that our teens and young adult believers are confused about, which encouraged me to write this short booklet. When I was a teenager, even as a young adult in my twenties and thirties, I couldn't tell you how to be saved or why we needed to go to church. This booklet is not in-depth but is meant to serve as a guide in the right direction. I advise you to read your Bible and be amazed by the content inside.

Reflection is huge for our development in the Word of God. This workbook is not designed to create scholars but thinkers of the Word. Specifically, how and where the scriptures of the Bible apply in and around our lives. Reflect on each passage, question, and your life. Remember, we read to collect thoughts and reflect to connect thoughts. To read and not reflect is like chewing and not swallowing. Apply what you learn as you journey through this workbook because learning without application leads to stagnation, and stagnation leads to frustration. As you continuously use what you have learned in the Word, you will start to see a difference in your outlook on life. Repetition builds competence, which leads to confidence. Wow, an understanding of God's Word will give me confidence in the Lord. Amen.

Table of Contents

About the Author 1

Message from the Author 2

Lesson 1
Acknowledge Your Need for Salvation 4

Lesson 2
The Consequences of Sin 7

Lesson 3 10

Lesson 4 15

Lesson 5 18

Lesson 6 23

Lesson 7 26

Lesson 8
Purpose and Role of the Church 29

Lesson 1
Acknowledge Your Need for Salvation

The fact that you are reading this book leads me to believe that you realize God is real and that you need to be saved from eternal hell. Acknowledging your need for salvation is the first step toward a relationship with God. It begins with recognizing the reality of sin and its consequences. The Bible teaches that all have sinned and fallen short of God's glory (Romans 3:23), creating a separation between humanity and God. This separation leads to spiritual death (Romans 6:23). By understanding this need (to be saved by God), we become aware of our dependence on God and the necessity of being saved. Many people are not sure about how to be saved. Even many Christians have a challenging time explaining how to be saved. Throughout Part One of this book, you'll discover directions to salvation.

Sin

What is sin? To put it simply, disobedience to God. The Bible, cover to cover, is filled with many directives, commands, and exhortations. The only way to know how to obey Him is to read the Word of God, the Bible. More eloquently put, sin, according to the Bible, is any action, thought, or attitude that goes against God's will, character, or laws. It is a violation of God's perfect standards and an act of rebellion against Him. According to 1 John 3:4, everyone who sins is breaking God's law, for all sin is contrary to the law of God. Sin is both a condition of the human heart and the actions that flow from it. In short, sin is death.

These adjustments aim to enhance the clarity and flow of the text while maintaining the author's original intent and style.

Discussion

<u>Definition and Understanding of Sin:</u>

- How would you personally define sin?
- Why do you think the Bible describes sin as both a condition and an action?
- How does viewing sin as a form of rebellion against God change the way we approach our own behavior?

<u>Biblical Insights on Sin:</u>

- 1 John 3:4 states, "Everyone who sins is breaking God's law." What do you think this means in practical terms?
- How do other Bible verses shape our understanding of what sin is and its consequences?

<u>The Nature of Sin and the Human Heart:</u>

- In what ways do you see sin as a condition of the heart rather than just a series of actions?
- How can we identify and address the root causes of sin in our lives?

<u>Impact of Sin on Relationships:</u>

- How does sin affect our relationship with God?
- In what ways does sin impact our relationships with others?

<u>Overcoming Sin:</u>

- What role does repentance play in addressing sin?
- How can we rely on God's grace and strength to overcome sinful tendencies?
- What practical steps can we take to align more closely with God's will?

<u>Reflections on God's Standards:</u>

- How do God's perfect standards challenge or inspire you in your daily life?
- How can we discern God's will in situations where sin may not be immediately obvious?

Lesson 2
The Consequences of Sin

In this section, we will take a very short venture into the arrival of sin. Sin affects us individually when it is present in our lives and has a generational impact. Knowledge of the origin of sin is very important for illustrating those mentioned above. I urge you to read Genesis chapters one through three.

The first sin on earth was committed by both Adam and Eve. Yes, Satan also sinned against God, but that is a story for another book to explain. I will give a little context for those unfamiliar with what happened. God prepared a place for man and woman to live, work, play, and rest. God gave them every kind of seed-bearing plant and tree to eat from. God gave them several commands, giving them free will to obey. In Genesis 1:28, God told them to be fruitful and multiply, to fill the earth and govern it, and to reign over the fish in the sea, the birds in the sky, and all the animals that scurry along the ground. The LORD God placed Adam in the Garden of Eden to tend and watch over it (work it and keep it). But the LORD God warned him, "You may freely eat the fruit of every tree in the garden, except the tree of the knowledge of good and evil."

Adam was given a wife, Eve, as a helper. While both Adam and Eve were in the garden, they were approached by Satan. After listening to Satan, both Adam and Eve ate from the one tree they were warned not to eat from. This was mankind's first act of disobedience toward God. The result of their disobedience led to them being removed from the garden, increased labor to provide for themselves, conflict within marriage regarding who takes charge, and pains during birth. The most important consequence was the separation from God. There was a spiritual death that took place, removing the close communion once shared with God. Now, all are born without a spiritual connection with God. It is not until we receive salvation that we are reconnected to God through the Holy Spirit, which is given to us upon becoming a child of God. The previous sentence will be explained in further detail within the following few sections of the book.

Discussion

<u>Understanding the Context:</u>

- Why is it important to know the origin of sin as described in Genesis chapters 1–3?
- How does the account of Adam and Eve's disobedience help illustrate the concept of sin's generational impact?

<u>God's Instructions and Human Choice:</u>

- What was the significance of God's command not to eat from the tree of the knowledge of good and evil?
- How does the concept of free will play a role in the first sin?
- Why do you think Adam and Eve chose to listen to Satan despite God's warning?

<u>Consequences of Sin:</u>

- How did Adam and Eve's disobedience affect their relationship with God?
- In what ways did their sin lead to changes in their daily lives (work, relationships, childbirth)?
- What does the separation from God in the garden symbolize for all of humanity?

<u>The Role of Satan:</u>

- What can we learn from the way Satan tempted Adam and Eve?
- How might understanding Satan's role in the first sin help us identify and resist temptation in our own lives?

<u>Sin's Ongoing Impact:</u>

- What does it mean that we are all born without a spiritual connection with God?
- How does receiving salvation restore that connection?
- What lessons can we apply from this passage to our own spiritual journey and daily choices?

Lesson 3

What Is a Lord?

The concept of a lord is foreign to many Americans, including me. Traditionally, a lord was a person who held a position of power, authority, or nobility, often a title within a monarchical system. Lords were figures of social authority in their regions. They often administered justice and served as the local representative of the king. Lords ruled over a specific area, aligning their laws with the king's laws. People under their lordship were expected to obey the laws and ways of doing things as set by the lord.

To Confess Is to Accept His Lordship

Romans 10:9 states, "If you openly declare that Jesus is Lord and believe in your heart that God raised him from the dead, you will be saved." To declare is to confess that Jesus is Lord—specifically, your Lord! Therefore, if you declare He is your Lord, you are accepting His lordship over you. This means you accept His authority over you! You will obey all His commands and expectations because He is your Lord! This means His will is now your will.

If someone were to confess or declare Jesus is Lord and doesn't obey Him, then they have not accepted His lordship. This means they have not truly declared Him as Lord and, therefore, do NOT have salvation. To be frank, they are going to hell! In Luke 6:46, Jesus asks, "So why do you keep calling me 'Lord, Lord!' when you don't do what I say?" In Matthew 7:21, Jesus states, "Not everyone who calls out to me, 'Lord! Lord!' will enter the Kingdom of Heaven. Only those who actually do the will of my Father in heaven will enter." Jesus is under the authority of His Father, Abba, in heaven, and we are under the authority of Jesus. Therefore, when we accept His lordship, we begin to abide in His will, which is the Father's will.

We must begin to give up our ways for His ways. Remove temporal pleasures that are not aligned with His will. Follow His examples and teachings in His word. Most importantly, obey Him. (Hint: you must read His word to know how to obey Him.) The second part of Romans 10:9, "believe in your heart that God raised him from the dead," means to believe Jesus died for your sins. This means you realize that you must repent (turn away from your sinful ways and ask for forgiveness of your sins) because Jesus gave Himself as a perfect sacrifice for your sins. Acts 3:19 tells us, "Now repent of your sins and turn to God, so that your sins may be wiped away."

Become a Child of God

First, you must confess that Jesus is Lord. It's okay if you do not fully understand what this means. Your local church is responsible for guiding you in this process, so find one near you. Next, believe in your heart that God raised Jesus from the dead. This is to believe Jesus died for your sins and was raised from the dead, cleansing you of all your sins as you ask for His forgiveness. This is what it means to believe. The Bible is one document that supports itself from cover to cover. As you begin to read the Bible, you will see different verses that refer to salvation by solely believing. It does not contradict Romans 10:9 but rather summarizes it. To believe means you believe Jesus is your Lord, accepting His lordship over you and that He died for your sins to be raised with all authority as your Savior.

John 1:12 tells us that all who believed Him and accepted Him, He gave the right to become children of God. Because we are His children, God has sent the Spirit of His Son into our hearts (Galatians 4:6). Ephesians 1:13 tells us that when we believed in Christ, He identified us as His own by giving us the Holy Spirit, whom He promised long ago.

Discussion

<u>What Does It Mean to Call Jesus "Lord"?</u>

- How does the traditional concept of a lord help us understand what it means to confess Jesus as Lord?
- What responsibilities do we take on when we accept Jesus' lordship over our lives?

<u>Confession and Obedience:</u>

- Why do you think Romans 10:9 connects confessing Jesus as Lord with salvation?
- How would you respond to someone who declares Jesus as Lord but struggles to obey His commands?
- What do Jesus' statements in Luke 6:46 and Matthew 7:21 teach us about the relationship between calling Him "Lord" and doing His will?

<u>The Role of Faith in Salvation:</u>

- What does it mean to "believe in your heart that God raised Him from the dead"?
- How do repentance and belief in Jesus' sacrifice fit together in the process of becoming a child of God?

<u>Living Under Jesus' Lordship:</u>

- What are some practical ways we can "give up our ways for His ways"?
- How does reading and understanding the Bible help us live under Jesus' authority?

<u>The Assurance of Becoming a Child of God:</u>

- According to John 1:12 and Galatians 4:6, what changes when we believe and accept Jesus as Lord?
- How does receiving the Holy Spirit affirm our new identity as children of God?

Challenges and Encouragements:

- Why is it sometimes challenging to fully submit to Jesus' lordship in every area of our lives?
- What encouragements from Scripture or personal experience have helped you trust in Jesus' authority?

Lesson 4

Live a Transformed Life

According to 2 Corinthians 5:17, "Anyone who belongs to Christ has become a new person. The old life is gone; a new life has begun!"

Filled with the Spirit

Peter was a man who walked with Jesus. He witnessed all the amazing miracles Jesus performed, from feeding thousands with little, to healing the sick, casting out demons, raising the dead, giving sight to the blind, enabling the lame to walk, and cleansing lepers. Let's not forget the times Jesus defied the laws of nature by walking on water and rebuking the storm, all of which Peter witnessed. Despite all that Peter had seen, when Jesus was taken away, a servant girl asked, "Weren't you with Jesus?" Peter denied being with Jesus three times. He didn't even have the courage to claim Jesus in front of a little servant girl, as Paul Washer would put it.

Many believers were present on the day of Pentecost (a festival) and received the Holy Spirit. Thousands of Jews heard the commotion and came to see what was taking place. Peter, the same man who was afraid to claim Christ in front of a little servant girl, stepped forward and began to preach to thousands. These were the same men who crucified the Savior, Jesus Christ, that Peter was speaking to.

What was the difference? Peter had received the Holy Spirit. The power and courage of the Holy Spirit spoke through Peter. Peter continued on other occasions, chastising those who came against Jesus and preaching repentance. On one occasion, 3,000 men were saved, and on another occasion, 5,000 men were saved as a result of Peter, who was now filled with the Holy Spirit, preaching and teaching Christ to the lost. Once you are saved, you are filled with the Holy Spirit. It changes your heart and your desires.

Discussion

<u>Understanding Transformation in Christ:</u>

- How does 2 Corinthians 5:17 define the change that happens when someone belongs to Christ?
- What are some ways you've experienced this new life in your own walk with God?

<u>Peter's Transformation:</u>

- What do you think caused Peter to deny Jesus before receiving the Holy Spirit?
- How did the Holy Spirit's presence transform Peter's courage and ability to share the Gospel?
- In what ways can we relate to Peter's initial fear and eventual boldness?

<u>The Role of the Holy Spirit:</u>

- How does the Holy Spirit influence a believer's heart and desires?
- Why is it important to rely on the Holy Spirit when sharing our faith or making daily decisions?

<u>Evidence of a Changed Life:</u>

- What are some outward signs that a person is living a transformed, Spirit-filled life?
- How can we continue to grow in our relationship with God after experiencing salvation?

<u>Sharing the Gospel:</u>

- Peter went from denying Jesus to preaching to thousands. What does this teach us about God's power to use us despite our past failures?
- What role does the Holy Spirit play in empowering us to share the Gospel boldly today?

Lesson 5

Guided by the Bible

Now that you are filled with the Holy Spirit, you must walk in the Holy Spirit. To walk is to live. The only way you will know how you are supposed to live and what you are supposed to do according to God's will is to read His word. We learn in 2 Timothy 3:16-17 that "All Scripture is inspired by God and is useful to teach us what is true and to make us realize what is wrong in our lives. It corrects us when we are wrong and teaches us to do what is right. God uses it to prepare and equip his people to do every good work." Another verse of the Bible that gives reason to read the Word of God is Romans 15:4, which states, "Such things were written in the Scriptures long ago to teach us. And the Scriptures give us hope and encouragement as we wait patiently for God's promises to be fulfilled."

Use the Bible as your guide in life! Not social media, not gospel music, not even sermons. Sermons are made to support the Word of God, not be held higher than the Word of God. Many new and young believers fail to rely on the reading of the Word and rely more on the preaching of the Word. Both are needed, but one is more important than the other.

Walking in the Spirit

Walking in the Spirit refers to living a life guided and empowered by the Holy Spirit, which is the presence of God in a believer's life. Walking in the Spirit means aligning your thoughts, actions, and decisions with God's will, as Scripture reveals. It involves seeking to obey God and live in a way that reflects His character. An example is choosing kindness, patience, and forgiveness over anger or revenge because these reflect the fruits of the Spirit (Galatians 5:22-23).

This includes relying on the Holy Spirit for strength, guidance, and wisdom rather than depending solely on your own efforts or understanding. This includes praying for the Spirit's help. In biblical terms, the "flesh" represents the sinful nature or desires that go against God's ways. Walking in the Spirit involves resisting these desires and living in holiness. Galatians 5:16 says, "So I say, walk by the Spirit, and you will not gratify the desires of the flesh." A life lived in the Spirit will naturally exhibit characteristics of the Spirit, known as the "fruit of the Spirit": love, joy, peace, patience, kindness, goodness, faithfulness, gentleness, and self-control (Galatians 5:22-23). Walking in the Spirit requires being spiritually alert and attuned to God's direction. This involves praying and meditating, reading and applying Scripture, and listening for God's guidance in your heart.

To walk in the Spirit is to imitate Christ in every area of life, allowing the Spirit to shape your character and actions to reflect His love and righteousness. Examples are choosing to pray or seek God's guidance before deciding, offering grace and forgiveness when someone has wronged you, and serving others selflessly and with humility.

Discussion

<u>The Importance of Scripture:</u>

- Why is it essential to rely on the Bible as your primary guide in life?
- How does 2 Timothy 3:16-17 describe the benefits of reading and applying Scripture?
- What role does the Bible play in shaping our understanding of God's will?

<u>Scripture vs. Other Resources:</u>

- Why should we prioritize God's Word over social media, gospel music, or sermons?
- How can we ensure that sermons and other Christian resources support rather than replace our personal study of Scripture?

<u>Walking in the Spirit:</u>

- What does it mean to "walk in the Spirit" in everyday life?
- How can you tell if you're living according to the Spirit rather than following the desires of the flesh?
- What steps can you take to align your thoughts, actions, and decisions with God's will?

<u>The Fruit of the Spirit:</u>

- What characteristics make up the "fruit of the Spirit" according to Galatians 5:22-23?
- How do these characteristics show that someone is living a Spirit-led life?
- Which of these fruits do you find most challenging to exhibit, and how can the Holy Spirit help you grow in that area?

Practical Applications:

- What practical habits help you remain spiritually alert and attuned to God's direction?
- How do prayer and meditation on Scripture help you walk in the Spirit?
- Share an example from your own life where choosing to walk in the Spirit made a difference in how you responded to a difficult situation.

Lesson 6

Obey the Word of God

Matthew 24:12–13 teaches that sin will be rampant everywhere, and the love of many will grow cold. But the one who endures to the end will be saved. Salvation is not a one-and-done action. Persistence is essential; though we as Christians may fall away, it is vital to realign ourselves on the path of righteousness.

The Greatest Command

If a believer is not familiar with the greatest command, then they are consistently failing the Father, our God. I was 35 years old before learning God's greatest command. That is years of not obeying God's command because I did not find the importance of knowing His word. In Matthew 22:37–38, Jesus said, "You must love the Lord your God with all your heart, all your soul, and all your mind. This is the first and greatest commandment." Loving God with all your heart, soul, and mind means prioritizing God above all else and being fully devoted to Him in thought, emotion, and action. It involves worship, obedience, trust, and seeking a personal relationship with Him. In John 14:23, Jesus shared, "All who love me will do what I say. My Father will love them, and we will come and make our home with each of them. Anyone who doesn't love me will not obey me." Here, Jesus tells us how to obey the first and greatest command. He makes it clear that love is an action. 1 John 3:18 also supports love to be an action as it states, "Dear children, let's not merely say that we love each other; let us show the truth by our actions."

Discussion

Understanding the Greatest Command:

- Why do you think Jesus called loving God with all your heart, soul, and mind the "greatest commandment"?
- What does it look like in everyday life to love God with all your heart, soul, and mind?
- How does prioritizing God help us remain on the path of righteousness?

Love as Action:

- How does Jesus' teaching in John 14:23 connect love for Him with obedience?
- In what ways can we demonstrate our love for God through our actions, not just words?
- How does 1 John 3:18 challenge us to live out our faith in practical, visible ways?

Endurance in Faith:

- What challenges can cause believers to "fall away" from following God's commands?
- How can we persist in our faith and obedience even when it's difficult?
- What role does knowing and meditating on Scripture play in helping us endure to the end?

The Impact of Knowing God's Word:

- How did learning about the greatest command later in life change the way you approached your relationship with God?
- Why is it important for believers to seek out and understand God's commands early in their faith journey?
- How can we encourage others to discover and follow God's commands in a way that deepens their love and trust in Him?

Lesson 7

The Great Commission

Once you are saved, it is your responsibility to continue the work of Jesus, which is to spread the word and make believers. We were not just saved to have a spot in heaven; we were saved to join in on the work of Jesus by building the body of Christ, specifically increasing the number of believers. The goal is for us, as believers, to help save as many people as we can.

The Great Commission is the instruction Jesus gave to His disciples after His resurrection, commanding them to spread the message of the Gospel to all people around the world. A disciple is someone who follows and spreads the teachings of another. Jesus told His disciples to go and make disciples of all nations, baptizing them in the name of the Father, the Son, and the Holy Spirit (Matthew 28:18–20).

Evidence of Faith

A life transformed by God evidences true faith. In comparison, salvation is by grace through faith (Ephesians 2:8–9); the outward evidence of that faith is seen in obedience, good works, and spiritual fruit. These signs don't earn salvation but prove a genuine relationship with God. James 2:17 tells us that faith by itself isn't enough. Unless it produces good deeds, it is dead and useless.

Discussion

<u>Understanding the Mission:</u>

- Why is it important for believers to take an active role in the Great Commission?
- What does it mean to "make disciples of all nations"?

<u>Personal Responsibility:</u>

- How can you personally contribute to spreading the Gospel and making disciples?
- What are some practical ways to share the message of Jesus in your community or workplace?

<u>Faith and Evidence:</u>

- How do good deeds and spiritual fruit reflect a true relationship with God?
- What steps can you take to ensure that your faith is not just an inward belief, but also outwardly visible through your actions?

<u>Challenges and Encouragement:</u>

- What challenges might arise when sharing your faith, and how can you overcome them?
- How does knowing that you're part of God's plan to build His kingdom encourage you to be bold in your faith?

<u>The Impact of Obedience:</u>

- How can obedience to the Great Commission strengthen your own faith?
- What impact might our collective obedience have on the global church and future generations of believers?

Lesson 8
Purpose and Role of the Church

To Make Disciples

One of the most significant purposes the church serves is to edify believers. To edify means instructing, improving, guiding, encouraging, building up, strengthening, and supporting fellow believers in their faith and spiritual growth. Edification is a continuous process. We always have room for growth, support, and encouragement. The church is to make disciples, meaning the focus is not merely on conversion (this means the church is not made for merely saving people) but on discipleship—helping others grow in their faith, understand God's Word, and live in obedience to Jesus. Jesus tells his disciples to go and make disciples, then to teach the new disciples to obey all the commands He had given (Matthew 28:18–20).

Ephesians 4:11–12 states, "Now these are the gifts Christ gave to the church: the apostles, the prophets, the evangelists, and the pastors and teachers. Their responsibility is to equip God's people to do his work and build up the church, the body of Christ."

To Worship God

The primary reason for the church's existence is to bring glory to God. Ephesians 3:21 declares, "Glory to him in the church and in Christ Jesus through all generations forever and ever! Amen." Everything the church does—preaching, serving, fellowship, and missions—should point back to God and magnify His character.

The church gathers as a community to worship God together. Hebrews 10:25 teaches us not to give up meeting together, as some are in the habit of doing, but to encourage one another. Gathering to worship God reflects the eternal worship we will experience in heaven, where all nations and tongues glorify Him together (Revelation 7:9–10).

The Church Serves Others

The church serves its members by encouraging and supporting them, praying for and with one another as directed in James 5:16. The church does more than teach, mentor, and disciple members to grow in faith. The church serves the community by meeting practical needs and helping the poor, feeding the hungry, caring for the sick, and supporting the marginalized. The early church shared possessions to meet the needs of others (Acts 2:44–45).

Young believers, "you" must join in on God's work through His church. Our God, who grants eternal life, wipes our slate clean, calls us His own, and loves us like no other. Join me in the fight against the flesh, the world, and Satan. Join me in the struggle to bring the lost to Christ! To help believers stay on the narrow road to our Father in heaven.

Discussion

<u>Making Disciples:</u>

- What does it mean for the church to focus on discipleship rather than just conversion?
- How can we actively help other believers grow in their faith and obedience to Jesus?
- How does the church equip its members to become disciples who can then make more disciples?

<u>Worshiping God:</u>

- Why is bringing glory to God considered the church's primary purpose?
- In what ways does gathering for worship reflect the eternal worship described in Revelation 7:9–10?
- How can the church ensure that all its activities, from preaching to missions, truly point back to God?

<u>Serving Others:</u>

- How does the church serve both its members and the wider community?
- What are some examples from the early church (Acts 2:44–45) that we can apply today?
- Why is it important for the church to balance teaching and mentoring with practical acts of service?

<u>Our Role in the Church:</u>

- What does it mean for each believer to join in God's work through the church?
- How can individuals contribute to the church's mission of edification, worship, and service?
- What motivates you personally to be an active part of the church community?

Challenges and Encouragement:

- What challenges might the church face in fulfilling its mission, and how can we overcome them?
- How can the church encourage its members to stay faithful and persevere in their spiritual journey?
- How does being part of the church help us remain focused on the narrow path that leads to the Father?

www.ingramcontent.com/pod-product-compliance
Lightning Source LLC
LaVergne TN
LVHW072117060526
838201LV00011B/259